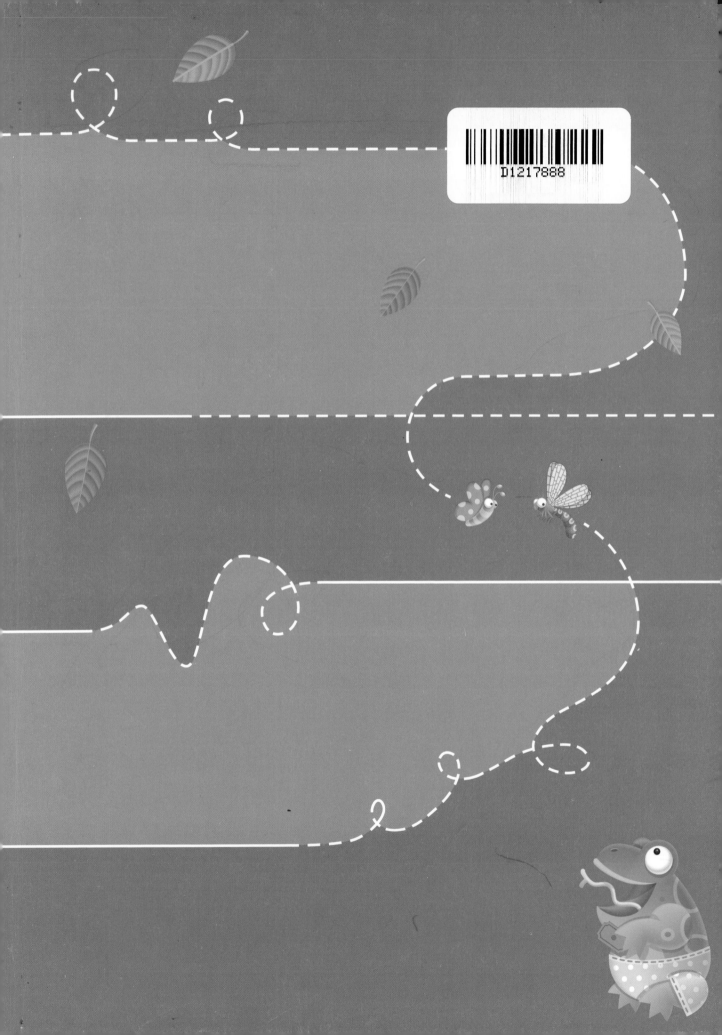

Program Authors

Peter Afflerbach

Camille Blachowicz

Candy Dawson Boyd

Wendy Cheyney

Connie Juel

Edward Kame'enui

Donald Leu

Jeanne Paratore

P. David Pearson

Sam Sebesta

Deborah Simmons

Sharon Vaughn

Susan Watts-Taffe

Karen Kring Wixson

PEARSON

Scott
Foresman

Editorial Offices: Glenview, Illinois • Parsippany, New Jersey • New York, New York
Sales Offices: Needham, Massachusetts • Duluth, Georgia • Glenview, Illinois
Coppell, Texas • Sacramento, California • Mesa, Arizona

We dedicate Reading Street to
Peter Jovanovich.

⌒

His wisdom, courage,
and passion for education
are an inspiration to us all.

About the Cover Artist

Daniel Moreton lives in New York City, where he uses his computer to create illustrations for books. He has two dogs—basset hounds named Zoey and Eddie. Can you find Eddie on the cover of this book?

ISBN: 0-328-10831-6

3 4 5 6 7 8 9 10 V063 14 13 12 11 10 09 08 07 06

Dear Reader,

What interesting things have you learned in your travels down *Scott Foresman Reading Street?* What interesting people have you met along the way?

In this book you will read about treasures. What things do you treasure? We hope you will treasure the stories and articles that we have included in this book. They are about surprising treasures and treasures we share!

Have fun exploring the interesting information you will find on *Scott Foresman Reading Street!*

Sincerely,
The Authors

Read It
ONLINE
sfsuccessnet.com

Treasures

What do we treasure?

Surprising Treasures

Treasures to Share

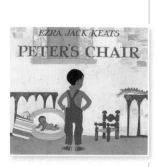

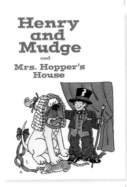

Treasures

What do we treasure?

9

Let's Talk About
Surprising Treasures

Words to Read

give
surprise
would
enjoy
worry
about

12

Read the Words

Francisco wants to give his mother a surprise party. Francisco thinks she would enjoy it. But he does worry that she will find out about the party. Can he surprise her?

Genre: Realistic Fiction
Realistic fiction is a made-up story that could really happen. Next you will read about a birthday surprise.

Mama's Birthday Present

by Carmen Tafolla

illustrated by Gabriel Pacheco

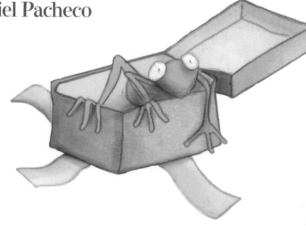

What is Mama's birthday present?

Francisco ran into the garden.
His grandmother was reading a book.

16

"Grandma! Grandma!" called Francisco.
"Next Sunday is Mama's birthday! Mama
always surprises me with a party for my
birthday. Can we surprise Mama with a party?"

"That is a wonderful idea, Francisco," said Grandma. "Today is Monday. If we begin today, we will have seven days to plan a party."

"Mama always gives me a present for my birthday," said Francisco. "What present can I give Mama?"

"I don't know," said Grandma. "But don't worry. We can make a piñata to break. Your mama will enjoy that."

So Grandma and Francisco made a piñata.

On Tuesday, Francisco wondered about
Mama's present. Francisco went to talk with
Papa about Mama's birthday party.

"What present can I give Mama?"
asked Francisco.

"I don't know," said Papa. "But don't worry. I can play my guitar. Your mama will enjoy that."

So Papa promised Francisco he would play his guitar.

On Wednesday, Francisco wondered about Mama's present. Francisco and his older brother went to invite Señora Molina to Mama's party. Señora Molina had a tortilla shop.

"What present can I give Mama?" asked Francisco.

"I don't know," said Señora Molina. "But don't worry. I can bring some hot tortillas, fresh off the stove. Your mama will enjoy that."

So Señora Molina promised Francisco she would bring hot tortillas, fresh off the stove.

On Thursday, Francisco wondered about
Mama's present. He went to talk to his friend
Gina about it.

"What present can I give Mama?"
asked Francisco.

"I don't know," said Gina. "But don't worry. We can make confetti eggs to crack on people's heads. Your mama will enjoy that."

So Gina and Francisco filled and painted the bright confetti eggs.

On Friday, Francisco wondered about Mama's present. So he went to speak to Grandpa Pérez.

"What present can I give Mama?" asked Francisco.

"I don't know," said Grandpa Pérez.
"But don't worry. We can make some
sweet buñuelos. Your mama will enjoy that."
So Francisco and Grandpa Pérez made
some sweet buñuelos.

On Saturday, Francisco still wondered about his present for Mama. But Francisco had many things to do.

He helped his brothers
and sisters look for a place
to hang the piñata.

He talked to Papa
about the songs Papa
would play on his guitar.

He talked to Señora Molina
about the tortillas she would bring.

He found a
safe place to hide
Gina's confetti eggs

and Grandpa Pérez's
sweet buñuelos.

Everyone was ready for Mama's surprise.

On Sunday, everyone came to the party. Mama was very surprised.

Papa played his guitar. Señora Molina's hot tortillas smelled wonderful. Grandpa's sweet buñuelos tasted wonderful.

Everyone ate and sang and had fun. The children cracked confetti eggs over everyone's heads. Then they all lined up to take a swing at the piñata.

Everyone looked happy. Everyone
except Francisco.

"Francisco, what is the matter?"
asked Mama.

"I did not know what to give you for your
birthday, Mama."

"Oh, Francisco," said Mama. "This party was the best present you could give me. No, the second best."

"Second best?" asked Francisco.

"Yes. The best present of all is having my family and friends here with me. That is the most wonderful part of a party!"

Mama gave Francisco a big hug. Then they all took turns hitting the piñata. The one who broke it was Francisco.

And Mama enjoyed that.

Think and Share

Talk About It "Don't worry," everyone says to Francisco. What advice would you have given him about what to give Mama?

1. Use the pictures below to retell the story.

2. Why was a gift for Mama so important to Francisco?

3. Did you stumble on any words in the story? What did you do about it? How did you know what *buñuelos* are?

Look Back and Write What did everyone do at the party? Look back at pages 32–33. Make a list.

Carmen Tafolla

Carmen Tafolla grew up in San Antonio, Texas. She tells stories and writes poems about her Mexican American neighborhood.

Dr. Tafolla works with schools around the world to help children of all races and languages to succeed. She lives in a 100-year-old house in San Antonio with her husband, son, mother, and lots of books.

Read more books about treasures.

Chinese Surprises

by Annie Brannan

Do you ever eat Chinese food? If so, then you may know about these Chinese desserts. Inside each one is a small note. The note's message sometimes gives advice.

If you take time to laugh, you would enjoy life more.

Don't worry. Work hard and good things will happen.
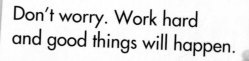

40

Sometimes a note tells about something that could happen to you.

Some day soon you will take a long trip.

Good things come to those who wait.

Why do people like these little desserts so much? People enjoy surprises!

Read Together

Adjectives

An **adjective** tells about a person, place, animal, or thing.

tall man

cute puppy

shaggy dog

42

Write Using Adjectives

1. Write these sentences. Circle each adjective.

Grandpa made sweet buñuelos.
Señora Molina made hot tortillas.

· ·

2. Write a sentence about a party. Use an adjective. Circle the adjective.

· ·

3. Plan a party! Write about the food you will serve. Use adjectives that tell people how good the food will be.

Let's Talk About Surprising Treasures

44

45

Words to Read

| draw |
| colors |
| over |
| drew |
| great |
| sign |
| show |

46

Read the Words

In art class we draw with pencils. Then we mix colors and paint over the drawings. I drew a great big cat. Let me sign it. Then I will show it to you.

The Dot

Genre: Realistic Fiction
Realistic fiction stories are made up, but they have characters that seem real. In the next story you will see what happens to one small dot.

The Dot

by Peter H. Reynolds

How can a dot be a treasure?

49

Art class was over, but Vashti sat glued to her chair. Her paper was empty.

Vashti's teacher leaned over the blank paper.
"Ah! A polar bear in a snowstorm," she said.
"Very funny!" said Vashti. "I just CAN'T draw!"

Her teacher smiled. "Just make a mark and see where it takes you."

Vashti grabbed a marker and gave the paper a good, strong jab. "There!"

Her teacher picked up the paper and studied it carefully. "Hmmmmm."

She pushed the paper toward Vashti and quietly said, "Now sign it."

Vashti thought for a moment.
"Well, maybe I can't draw, but I
CAN sign my name."

The next week, when Vashti walked into art class, she was surprised to see what was hanging above her teacher's desk.

It was the little dot she had drawn—HER DOT! All framed in swirly gold!

"Hmmph! I can make a
better dot than THAT!"

She opened her never-before-used
set of watercolors and set to work.
Vashti painted and painted.

A red dot.
A purple dot.
A yellow dot.
A blue dot.

The blue mixed with the yellow. She
discovered that she could make a GREEN dot.

Vashti kept experimenting.
Lots of little dots in many colors.

"If I can make little dots, I can make BIG dots too." Vashti splashed her colors with a bigger brush on bigger paper to make bigger dots.

Vashti even made a dot
by NOT painting a dot.

At the school art show a few weeks later,
Vashti's *many dots made quite a splash*.

Vashti noticed a little boy
gazing up at her.

"You're a really great artist.
I wish I could draw," he said.

"I bet you can," said Vashti.
"ME? No, not me. I can't draw
a straight line with a ruler."

Vashti smiled. She handed the boy a blank sheet of paper. "Show me."

The boy's pencil shook as he drew his line.

Vashti stared at the boy's squiggle.
And then she said . . .

"Sign it."

Think and Share

Talk About It Vashti didn't think she could draw. How did her teacher help her? Has anything like this happened to you? Explain.

1. Which picture below is out of order? Where should it be? Use the pictures to retell the story.

2. What is the big idea of *The Dot*? What lesson did you learn?

3. Make a story map of *The Dot.*

Look Back and Write Look back at page 60. How does Vashti make a dot by not painting a dot?

Meet the Author and Illustrator
Peter H. Reynolds

Peter Reynolds says *The Dot* "is a book that encourages us to be brave about expressing ourselves. It gently reminds us to start small and explore the idea."

Mr. Reynolds collects ideas for stories in his journal. He likes to doodle on scraps of paper. He collects these little drawings in old tin boxes.

Read more books by Peter H. Reynolds.

A Great Artist and His Dots

by Karen Stockwell

Georges Seurat liked to draw in the park.

He drew people and animals.

He painted lots of dots over his drawings.

The dots were many colors.

One huge painting he signed shows
ladies and men in a park.
Now this beautiful painting is in a museum.
People come to see it each day.

Adjectives for Colors and Shapes

Some **adjectives** name colors.

Some **adjectives** name shapes.

green dot   **yellow** dot   **blue** dot

round dot   **straight** line   **square** frame

 Write Using Adjectives for Shapes and Colors

1. Write these sentences. Circle each adjective.

Vashti painted a red dot.
The boy drew a square house.

. . . .

2. Write a sentence about a picture you painted. Use adjectives for colors and shapes. Circle the adjectives.

. . . .

3. Write about an object you want to buy. Use adjectives for shapes and colors. Circle the adjectives.

Let's Talk About
Surprising
Treasures

Words to Read

once
wild
found
took
mouth

Read the Words

Once the wild T. Rex roamed the West. But not any more. T. Rex bones have been found in many places. Workers took the bones and put them together. Look at that mouth! Those teeth are sharp.

Genre: Biography
A biography is the story of a real person's life. Next you will read about Barnum Brown, an interesting man.

Mister Bones

Mister Bones

Dinosaur Hunter

by Jane Kurtz
illustrated by Mary Haverfield

What can animal
bones tell us?

Smooth Barnum Brown
was a charming, dapper guy.

He went climbing over rocks
in a topcoat and a tie.

He loved ballroom dancing, but he was not dancing now. He was digging in the dirt. What was he looking for? It was not shining silver. His wife once called it rainbows, but it was not in the sky.

Others wore bandannas and cowboy boots and chaps. Mister Brown came to Montana in a fancy coat and hat.

He poked and he sifted and he picked in the dirt. Was he hunting gold? No, nothing quite that old.

But what he hunted, people wanted just
about as much as gold. Bones. Big old bones.

People said, "Barnum Brown can somehow smell bones." His nickname became Mister Bones.

Mister Bones found bones in the middle of Montana—a backbone and a hip bone and other bones and chips.

Bones were packed in boxes, shipped off to New York. Putting them together took lots and lots of work.

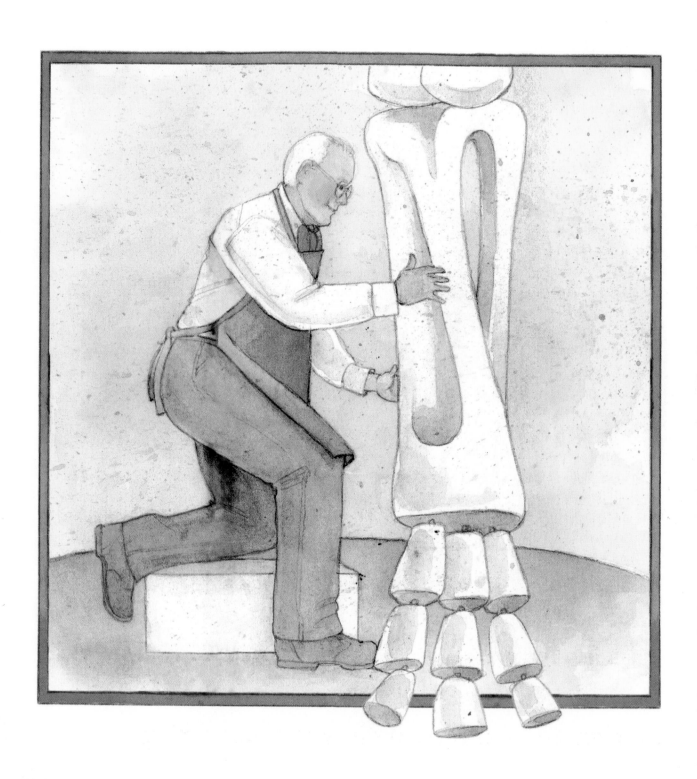

Step back! Imagine that! Now what about
a name? A name? Yes, a name for this
amazing thing.

That job went to the museum president.
Henry Osborn called it tyrant lizard king.

It was as tall as three men but had short, short arms. It had a wide, wild mouth and six-inch teeth.

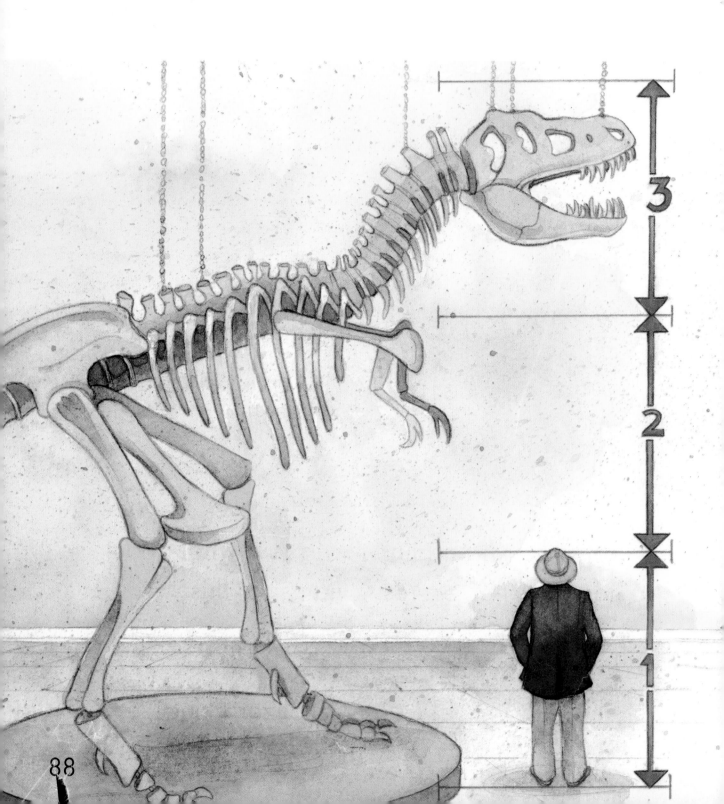

3

2

1

Huge Tyrannosaurus. Gigantic T. Rex. Mister Bones had found the tyrant lizard king.

Think and Share

Talk About It Old bones were treasures to Barnum Brown. What is a treasure to you?

1. Use the pictures to summarize what you learned about Barnum Brown.

2. Why do you think Jane Kurtz wrote *Mister Bones: Dinosaur Hunter?*

3. Henry Osborn called T. Rex a "tyrant lizard king." What is a tyrant? Use your glossary to find out.

Look Back and Write Look back at page 84. Could Barnum Brown really "smell bones"? What does the author mean?

Meet the Author
Jane Kurtz

Jane Kurtz has liked dinosaurs ever since her parents took her to Dinosaur National Monument when she was seven years old.

Ms. Kurtz did a lot of research for *Mister Bones.* "I had to learn lots and lots about Barnum Brown to find the most interesting facts to include. The research took months. The writing took only weeks."

Read more books by Jane Kurtz.

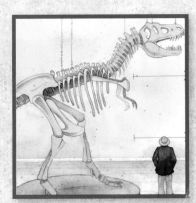

What's in a

by Mary Rowan

Museums are great places. At this museum, you can find out about art. You can mix colors. Once you have the colors you want, you can be an artist! Splash it on!

Museum ?

Where do the bones of a T. Rex go after they are found? They go to a museum! Workers took these bones and put them back together. Look at that mouth!

Some museums show you how things work. Look at this ball. Throw it up and watch it float. Why does it float? Experimenting with it helps you find out.

This museum shows where wild animals live. You can look in the windows and see their homes.

Visit a museum close to you. You can have loads of fun there!

Adjectives for Sizes

Some **adjectives** describe size.
The words **big, small, long,
short,** and **tiny** describe size.

T. Rex had **short** arms, a **wide** mouth,
and **huge** teeth.

The words **short, wide,** and **huge** help us
picture T. Rex.

Write Using Adjectives for Sizes

1. Write the sentences. Circle the adjectives that describe size.

Barnum Brown found big bones.
T. Rex was a large animal.

· ·

2. Write a sentence about a lizard or a dinosaur. Use an adjective for size. Circle the adjective.

· ·

3. Write about a pet you would like to get. Use adjectives that describe size. Circle the adjectives.

Let's Talk About

Treasures to Share

Words to Read

eight
moon
above
touch
laugh

Read the Words

All eight of us looked at the moon above us. It looked close enough to touch. This night was going to be fun. We began to laugh.

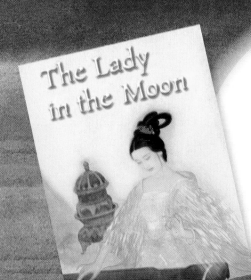

The Lady in the Moon

Genre: Realistic Fiction

Realistic fiction stories are made-up stories, but they tell about events that seem real. Next you will read about a special celebration.

The Lady in the Moon

by Lily Wong Fillmore

illustrated by Lin Wang

Who is the Lady in the Moon?

The sun sets. The moon rises.
Come out. Come out to play.
It is Moon Festival, a night
for children everywhere.

Let's sing a song to the Lady in the Moon.
Let's write a poem to send to Lady Moon.

We'll make some treats, good things to eat. We'll wrap them in lotus leaves, tied with golden knots.

Moon cakes, golden pears, melons, and plums.

We'll make eight treasures rice, wrapped in lotus leaves.

Night is falling, and children call,

"Come out, Lady Moon. Come light up the sky."

High above the city, high above the hills, the moon shows her golden face. Children sing and laugh. They send their poems to the Lady in the Moon.

She glows, she glides, she grows.
Lady Moon fills the sky with light.
Let's laugh and sing a song to Lady Moon.
Let's read our poems to Lady Moon.

We'll make her some treats,
good things to eat. We'll
wrap them in lotus leaves,
tied with golden knots.

Moon cakes,
golden pears,
melons, plums, and
eight treasures rice.

Raise your lanterns high. It is Moon Festival, a night for children everywhere. The moon is so near, you can touch it if you try. We light our lanterns. We raise them high.

Moon beams and
lanterns touch.
Oh, what a show!

A bridge of light glows
in the fall night.

113

Where does it go?
Will it take us to the moon?

Let's laugh and sing a song to Lady Moon.
Let's read our poems to the Lady in the Moon.
We'll take her some treats, good things to eat.

We'll wrap them
in lotus leaves,
tied with golden knots.

Moon cakes,
golden pears,
melons, plums, and
eight treasures rice.

Think and Share

Talk About It What part of the Moon Festival would be your favorite? Tell why.

1. Use the pictures below to retell important parts of *The Lady in the Moon.*

2. Is this story realistic or a fantasy? Tell why.

3. What did you wonder about as you read this story? What did you do to find out more?

Look Back and Write When is the Moon Festival celebrated? Look back at page 113.

Lily Wong Fillmore

As a child, Lily Wong Fillmore loved the Moon Festival. It was a time to eat fruits and moon cakes. It was a time to stay up late and have fun.

"If clouds got near the moon, we children were told to make a lot of noise," says Ms. Fillmore. "No one wanted clouds to cover the moon. It was the one night of the year we could play outdoors and make as much noise as we pleased."

Read more books about Asian celebrations.

My 4th of July

My family has fun on the 4th of July. Mom bakes eight pies to share at the block party.

We wrap red, white, and blue ribbons on our bikes.

We laugh as we try to win the sack race.

Dad knows the best place to watch the
fireworks at night. Crack! Bang! They light
up the sky above us.

Will the fireworks touch the moon? We laugh and cheer. What a beautiful sight!

Adjectives for What Kind

An **adjective** can tell what kind.
favorite day
dark sky
cool night

Happy children eat **sweet** treats.

Happy tells what kind of children.
Sweet tells what kind of treats.

Write Using Adjectives for What Kind

1. Write these sentences. Circle the adjectives for what kind.

It is a clear night.
There are bright stars in the sky.

. . . .

2. Write a sentence about the moon.
Use an adjective for what kind.
Circle the adjective.

. . . .

3. Write about a celebration
that you want others to come to.
Use adjectives for what kind.
Circle the adjectives.

Let's Talk About
Treasures to Share

Words to Read

stood
room
thought
picture
remember

Read the Words

Peter stood in his room.
He thought he would take down
his baby picture. Did anyone
remember when he was a baby?

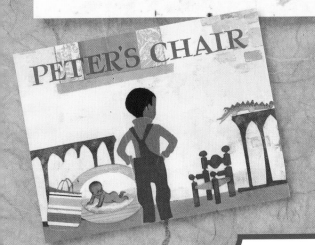

PETER'S CHAIR

Genre: Realistic Fiction

Realistic fiction has make-believe
characters who act like real
people. Next you will read about
a boy who has a new baby sister.

PETER'S CHAIR

by Ezra Jack Keats

What is special about Peter's chair?

Peter stretched as high as he could.
There! His tall building was finished.

CRASH! Down it came.

"Shhhh!" called his mother. "You'll have to play more quietly. Remember, we have a new baby in the house."

Peter looked into his sister Susie's room.
His mother was fussing around the cradle.

"That's my cradle," he thought, "and they
painted it pink!"

"Hi, Peter," said his father. "Would you like to help paint Sister's high chair?"
"It's my high chair," whispered Peter.

He saw his crib and muttered, "My crib. It's painted pink too."

Not far away stood his old chair.

"They didn't paint that yet!" Peter shouted.

He picked it up and ran to his room.

"Let's run away, Willie," he said. Peter filled
a shopping bag with cookies and dog biscuits.

"We'll take my blue chair, my toy crocodile, and the picture of me when I was a baby."

Willie got his bone.

They went outside and stood in
front of his house.

"This is a good place," said Peter.
He arranged his things very nicely and
decided to sit in his chair for a while.

But he couldn't fit in
the chair. He was too big!

His mother came to the window and called, "Won't you come back to us, Peter dear? We have something very special for lunch."

Peter and Willie made believe they didn't hear. But Peter got an idea.

Soon his mother saw signs that Peter was home. "That rascal is hiding behind the curtain," she said happily.

She moved the curtain
away. But he wasn't there!

"Here I am," shouted Peter.

Peter sat in a grown-up chair.
His father sat next to him.

"Daddy," said Peter, "let's paint the little chair pink for Susie."

And they did.

Think and Share

Talk About It Did you understand why Peter was sad? Have you ever felt as Peter did?

1. Use the pictures below to tell how Peter changed during the story.

2. Who are the characters in the story? Where does the story take place?

3. What is Peter's father doing at the beginning of the story? What is he doing at the end?

Look Back and Write Look back at pages 138–139. Make a list of what Peter and Willie take when they run away.

Meet the Author and Illustrator

Ezra Jack Keats

Ezra Jack Keats was an artist and author. He grew up in Brooklyn, New York, and often wrote about city life.

His first story about Peter, *The Snowy Day,* won the Caldecott Medal and made him famous. Mr. Keats died in 1983.

Read more books by Ezra Jack Keats.

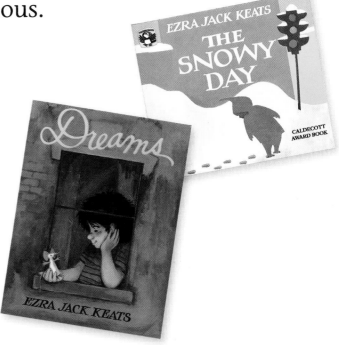

Peter's Baby Sister

Peter lives far from his grandmother.
They share news by e-mail. See how.

Write Reply Send Forward Delete Address Print

Hi, Grandma!

I have a new little sister.
I thought of a great idea.
Remember my little blue chair?
I painted it and stood it in her bedroom.
Please come to see us.

Peter

Then Peter clicks his mouse on the SEND button. In a flash, Grandma gets Peter's e-mail. Grandma reads Peter's e-mail. Then she writes back.

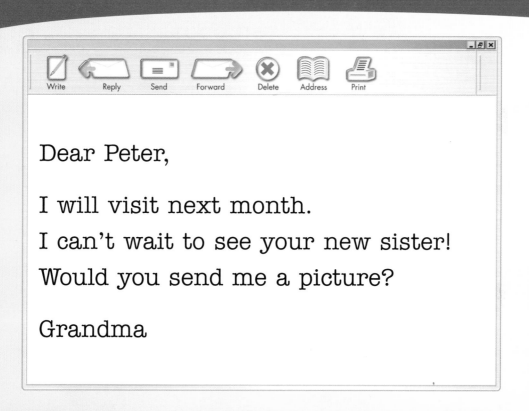

Dear Peter,

I will visit next month.
I can't wait to see your new sister!
Would you send me a picture?

Grandma

Grandma is glad to hear from Peter. Peter is glad to hear from Grandma. They like to share news by e-mail.

Adjectives for How Many

An **adjective** can tell how many.

six toys   **ten** dogs

Peter packed **five** cookies and **three** dog biscuits.

Five tells how many cookies. **Three** tells how many dog biscuits.

Write Using Adjectives for How Many

1. Write these sentences. Circle the adjectives for how many.

Peter has one sister.
Peter's chair has four legs.

· ·

2. Write a sentence that tells about your brothers, sisters, or friends. Use adjectives for how many. Circle the adjectives.

· ·

3. Write about what you would pack for a trip. Use adjectives for how many. Circle the adjectives.

Let's Talk About
Treasures to Share

Words to Read

told
only
across
because
dance
opened
shoes

Read the Words

Henry told Mudge they were only going across the street to Mrs. Hopper's house. They were staying with Mrs. Hopper because Mom and Dad were going to a dance. Mrs. Hopper opened the door. Henry walked in and took off his shoes.

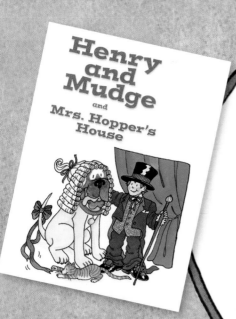

Henry and Mudge and Mrs. Hopper's House

Genre: Realistic Fiction
Realistic fiction has settings that seem real, but the stories are made up. Next you will find out what happens when Henry and Mudge visit a neighbor.

Henry and Mudge

and

Mrs. Hopper's House

by Cynthia Rylant

illustrated by Carolyn Bracken
in the style of Suçie Stevenson

What will Henry and Mudge
find at Mrs. Hopper's house?

A Sweetheart Dance

Valentine's Day was coming. Henry and his big dog Mudge loved Valentine's Day because of the candy. They liked the candy hearts that said "You're swell" and "Oh, dear" and things like that.

Henry read the words, and Mudge licked them off. They were a good team.

On this Valentine's Day Henry's father and Henry's mother were going to a Sweetheart Dance. Henry and Mudge would be staying with Mrs. Hopper.

Mrs. Hopper lived across the street in a big stone house with droopy trees and dark windows and a gargoyle on the door.

Henry liked Mrs. Hopper. But he did not like her house.

"Are you sure Mudge and I can't come to the Sweetheart Dance?" Henry asked his father.

"Only if you both promise to wear a tuxedo and shiny black shoes and waltz to 'The Blue Danube,'" said Henry's father.

Henry looked at Mudge and tried to imagine him in a tuxedo and shiny black shoes, waltzing to "The Blue Danube."

"I think we'd better go to Mrs. Hopper's," Henry said.

"Good idea," said Henry's father.

"Because Mudge only knows how to tap-dance," Henry said with a grin.

Costumes

Mrs. Hopper wasn't like anyone Henry had ever met. She played the violin for him. She served him tea. She told him about her father, who had been a famous actor.

She was very kind to Mudge. She cooked him a bowl of oatmeal and gave him his own loaf of French bread.

After the tea and music and oatmeal, Mrs. Hopper took them upstairs. She opened a room that had been her father's.

"Wow!" said Henry. The room was full
of costumes.

There were silk capes and tall hats and shiny coats. There were canes and swords and umbrellas. There were wigs.

Mrs. Hopper put a wig on Mudge.
"You look like a poodle, Mudge!"
said Henry.
Mudge wagged and wagged.

Henry and Mudge and Mrs. Hopper spent most of the evening in the costume room. They had a wonderful time.

And when Henry's parents came back from the dance, were they ever surprised. Mudge was a poodle, and Henry was a man! Henry wore a tuxedo and a hat and shiny black shoes.

178

"I bet you didn't know I was this handsome," Henry told his dad. And everyone laughed and laughed.

Think and Share

Talk About It Who do you think had a better time on Valentine's Day, Henry or his parents? Tell why you think as you do.

1. Use the pictures below to retell the story.

2. How did Mrs. Hopper come to have so many costumes?

3. This story has two chapters. How did the chapter titles help you as you read?

Test Practice

Look Back and Write Look back at page 176. What does Henry say Mudge looks like? Why does Henry think that?

Meet the Author
Cynthia Rylant

Cynthia Rylant grew up in West Virginia. She says, "I lived in a place called Cool Ridge, in a four-room house with my grandparents. We had no running water and my grandparents grew and hunted most of our food."

Ms. Rylant has written many books about Henry and Mudge. Now she lives in Oregon with her dogs Martha Jane and Gracie Rose.

Read more Henry and Mudge books.

Good Books, Good Times!

by Lee Bennett Hopkins
illustrated by Luciana Navarro Alves

Good books.
Good times.
Good stories.
Good rhymes.
Good beginnings.
Good ends.
Good people.
Good friends.
Good fiction.
Good facts.
Good adventures.
Good acts.
Good stories.
Good rhymes.
Good books.
Good times.

Dress-Up

by Bobbi Katz
illustrated by Luciana Navarro Alves

A treasure chest of castoff clothes!
    What's more fun, do you suppose?
With dandy costumes such as these
    we can dress up as we please!
A tie, a hat, a string of beads—
    are just the things that each kid needs!
Be a hunter or an elf—
    be *anyone* . . . except yourself!

Shell

by Myra Cohn Livingston
illustrated by Luciana Navarro Alves

When it was time
for Show and Tell,
Adam brought a big pink shell.

He told about
the ocean roar
and walking on the sandy shore.

And then he passed
the shell around.
We listened to the water sound.

And that's the first time
I could hear
the wild waves calling to my ear.

Reading

by Marchette Chute
illustrated by Luciana Navarro Alves

A story is a special thing.
The ones that I have read,
They do not stay inside the book,
They stay inside my head.

The Rainbow

by Iain Crichton Smith
illustrated by Luciana Navarro Alves

The rainbow's like a colored bridge
that sometimes shines from ridge to ridge.
Today one end is in the sea,
the other's in the field with me.

Adjectives That Compare

Some **adjectives** compare two or more persons, places, animals, or things. Add **-er** to an adjective to compare two persons, places, animals, or things.

That dog is **faster** than Mudge.

Add **-est** to an adjective to compare three or more persons, places, animals, or things.

Mudge is the **slowest** dog of all.

Write Using Adjectives That Compare

1. Add **-er** and **-est** to each of these adjectives.

   high   long   cold   warm   bright

. . . .

2. Write a sentence that compares how tall you are with how tall your teacher is. Use the correct adjective.

. . . .

3. Write about the zoo animals you think your class should see at the zoo. Use adjectives that compare to describe them.

A Favorite Celebration

connect to
WRITING

Francisco learned from his mother that a celebration with family and friends is a treasure. What celebration is a treasure to you? Write about it.
Tell why you treasure this special time.

A Celebration I Treasure

One day my brother and I planned

What do we treasure?

My Treasure

connect to
SOCIAL
STUDIES

Think of one thing that
is very special to you. Is it
something you can see and touch? Is it a
person or a pet? Tell a partner about it.
Explain why it is a treasure to you.

Something Old, Something New

connect to
SOCIAL
STUDIES

People like Barnum Brown in *Mr. Bones*
collect things that may seem odd to others.
Get together with a partner. Talk about why
old things may be as good as new things.
Make a chart to
show your ideas.

Treasures

Old Things | New Things

I Can Find the Answer

Where can you find the answers to questions you read?

In the Book

Sometimes the answers are RIGHT THERE in the book. You can put your finger right on the answer.

Right There

1. First, read the text.

2. Next, read the question and all the answer choices.

3. Then, look back at the text to find the answer.

Try It!

You might read this text and this question:

Su Lin liked to draw animals. She drew squirrels and birds. She drew lizards and crocodiles. Best of all, she liked to draw big elephants with long noses.

1 What does Su Lin like to draw most of all?

○ squirrels

○ lizards and crocodiles

○ elephants

Look back at the text.
The answer is RIGHT THERE.

Put your finger on the answer in the text.
Then put your finger on the right answer
to the question.

I Can Find the Answer

Where can you find the answers to questions?

Sometimes the answers are NOT right there in the text. You must read what the author wrote and use your head. You must FIGURE IT OUT!

Author and Me

1. First, read the text that the author wrote.

2. Next, read the question and all the answer choices.

3. Then, look back at the text to find clues.

4. Think about what YOU know.

5. Put this all together to FIGURE OUT the answer.

Try It!

You might read this text and this question:

It is time for the Moon Festival. Children laugh and play. They eat good treats. They join in to sing songs to Lady Moon.

1 How do the children feel at the Moon Festival?

○ sad

○ happy

○ cold

The text has clues that tell how the children feel.

You know that children are happy when they laugh, play, eat, and sing. You can use your head to FIGURE OUT the answer to the question.

Glossary

Aa

artist An **artist** is a person who makes art. **Artists** can make pictures and statues.

artist

Bb

bandannas **Bandannas** are large, colored handkerchiefs.

bandanna

biscuits **Biscuits** are small cakes that are not sweet.

buñuelos **Buñuelos** are sweet pastries that are fried and then covered with sugar. **Buñuelos** are like doughnuts, but smaller.

Cc

confetti **Confetti** is bits of colored paper thrown about during celebrations. We threw **confetti** at the birthday party.

cookies

cookies **Cookies** are small, flat, sweet cakes.

cowboy A **cowboy** is a person who works on a cattle ranch. **Cowboys** also take part in rodeos.

cradle A **cradle** is a small bed for a baby, usually one that can rock from side to side.

cowboy

crocodile

crocodile A **crocodile** is a large animal with thick skin, four short legs, and a pointed nose. **Crocodiles** look a lot like alligators.

curtain A **curtain** is a cloth or other material hung across a window. **Curtains** are often used to keep out light.

Ee

experimenting When you are **experimenting,** you are testing or trying something out. The cook is **experimenting** with new recipes.

Ff **festival** A **festival** is a special celebration. Some **festivals** include a parade.

festival

Gg **gargoyle** A **gargoyle** is a decoration. It usually is made of stone and shaped like a scary animal or person. **Gargoyles** often decorate buildings.

gargoyle

gigantic Something that is **gigantic** is like a giant. Gigantic things are very large and strong. Some dinosaurs were **gigantic.**

197

gold **Gold** is a bright yellow metal that is worth a lot of money. **Gold** is used to make jewelry and some coins.

guitar

guitar A **guitar** is a musical instrument that usually has six strings. You play a **guitar** with your fingers.

Hh

heart A **heart** is a figure shaped like this. ⟶ The card was covered with **hearts**.

heart

Ii

idea An **idea** is a thought or plan. It was my **idea** to go to the zoo.

Ll

lizard A **lizard** is a long, thin animal with dry, rough skin. **Lizards** look like very small crocodiles. Most **lizards** have four legs and a long tail.

lizard

lotus leaves **Leaves** are the flat, green parts of a tree or plant. A **lotus** is a water plant that has **leaves** and flowers.

Mm

Montana **Montana** is one of the fifty states of the United States.

museum A **museum** is a building for keeping and showing interesting things. People visit art **museums,** science **museums,** and **museums** with things from long ago.

Pp

pears **Pears** are sweet fruits that are round at one end. **Pears** are green or yellow and grow on trees.

pears

piñata

piñata A **piñata** is a decorated pottery pot filled with candy, fruit, and small toys. Blindfolded children swing sticks in order to break the **piñata** and get what is inside.

poem A **poem** is like a song without music. **Poems** often use words that rhyme. **Poems** sometimes put words together to tell about feelings and thoughts.

present

present A **present** is a gift. A **present** is something that someone gives you or that you give someone. His uncle sent him a birthday **present.**

200

Ss

shiny Something that is **shiny** is bright. Mom gave me a **shiny** new penny.

splash If you **splash** water or some other liquid, you cause it to fly around.

splash

squiggle

squiggle A **squiggle** is a wiggly twist or curve. The child drew a **squiggle** on the paper.

stared If you **stared,** you looked at someone with your eyes wide open for a long time. I **stared** at my sister.

straight If something is **straight,** it does not have a bend, turn, or curve. She drew a **straight** line. Try to stand up **straight.**

Tt

tortilla A **tortilla** is a thin, flat, round bread made of cornmeal. **Tortillas** are baked on a flat surface, filled with cheese or meat, and served hot.

treasures **Treasures** are things that are worth a lot. The pirates drew a map to show where the **treasures** were buried.

tuxedo

tuxedo A **tuxedo** is a formal suit for men. **Tuxedos** are usually black.

tyrant A **tyrant** is a mean, powerful ruler.

Vv **Valentine's Day** **Valentine's Day** is February 14, a day when people send cards with hearts and small presents.

Ww **waltz** To **waltz** means to dance slowly with graceful steps. Mom and Dad like to **waltz** together.

waltz

wonderful If something is **wonderful**, you like it very much. The ocean was a **wonderful** sight. She had a **wonderful** time at the party.

203

Tested Words

Mama's Birthday Present

about
enjoy
give
surprise
worry
would

The Dot

colors
draw
drew
great
over
show
sign

Mister Bones:
Dinosaur Hunter

found
mouth
once
took
wild

The Lady in the Moon

above
eight
laugh
moon
touch

Tested Words

Peter's Chair

picture
remember
room
stood
thought

Henry and Mudge and Mrs. Hopper's House

across
because
dance
only
opened
shoes
told

Acknowledgments

Text

Page 14: "Mama's Birthday Present" by Carmen Tafolla, 1991. Reprinted by permission of Carmen Tafolla.

Page 48: *The Dot* by Peter H. Reynolds. Copyright © 2003 by Peter H. Reynolds. Reproduced by permission of the publisher Candlewick Press, Inc., Cambridge, MA.

Page 76: Reprinted with the permission of Aladdin Paperbacks, an imprint of Simon & Schuster Children's Publishing Division from *Mister Bones: Dinosaur Hunter* by Jane Kurtz, illustrated by Mary Haverfield. Text copyright © 2004 Jane Kurtz. Illustrations copyright © 2004 Mary Haverfield.

Page 130: *Peter's Chair* by Ezra Jack Keats, 1967. © Ezra Jack Keats Foundation. Reprinted by permission.

Page 160: Reprinted with the permission of Simon & Schuster Books for Young Readers, an imprint of Simon & Schuster Children's Publishing from *Henry and Mudge and Mrs. Hopper's House* by Cynthia Rylant, illustrated by Carolyn Bracken in the style of Suçie Stevenson. Text copyright © 2003 Cynthia Rylant. Illustrations, Copyrights © 2002 by Suçie Stevenson. All rights reserved.

Page 182: "Good Books, Good Times!" from *Good Rhymes, Good Times* by Lee Bennett Hopkins. Copyright © 1995 by Lee Bennett Hopkins. First appeared in *Good Rhymes, Good Times* published by HarperCollins Publishers. Reprinted by permission of Curtis Brown, Ltd.

Page 183: "Dress-Up" from *Poems for Small Friends* by Bobbi Katz, copyright © 1989 by Random House, Inc. Illustrations © 1989 by Gyo Fujikawa. Used by permission of Random House Children's Books, a division of Random House, Inc.

Page 184: "Shell" by Myra Cohn Livingston. Reprinted with the permission of Margaret K. McElderry Books, an imprint of Simon & Schuster Children's Publishing Division, from *World's I Know and Other Poems* by Myra Cohn Livingston. Text, Copyright © 1985 by Myra Cohn Livingston. All rights reserved.

Page 185: "Reading" from *Rhymes About Us* by Marchette Chute. Published by E.P. Dutton & Co., 1974. Reprinted by permission of Elizabeth Hauser.

Page 185: "The Rainbow" by Iain Crichton Smith from *A Scottish Poetry Book,* 1983. Reprinted by permission of Carcanet Press Limited.

Illustrations

Cover: Daniel Moreton
14-36 Gabriel Pacheco
40-67 Peter H. Reynolds
70-83 Mary Haverfield
104-118 Lin Wang
118-136 Ezra Jack Keats
132, 183-185 Luciana Navarro Alves
146-165 Carolyn Bracken

Photographs

Every effort has been made to secure permission and provide appropriate credit for photographic material. The publisher deeply regrets any omission and pledges to correct errors called to its attention in subsequent editions.

Unless otherwise acknowledged, all photographs are the property of Scott Foresman, a division of Pearson Education.

Photo locators denoted as follows: Top (T), Center (C), Bottom (B), Left (L), Right (R), Background (Bkgd).

4 (TL) ©Georgette Douwma/Getty Images, (TL) ©Gary W. Carter/Corbis

8 (Bkgd) ©Dianna Sarto/Corbis, (TL) ©Georgette Douwma/Getty Images, (CL) ©Gary W. Carter/Corbis

10 ©Stewart Cohen/Index Stock Imagery

11 (BL) ©Jose Luis Pelaez, Inc./Corbis, (T) ©Royalty-Free/Corbis

69 Art Institute of Chicago, IL/Bridgeman Art Library

72 (Bkgd) ©Louie Psihoyos/Corbis, (CL) ©Melissa Farlow/NGS Image Collection

92 ©George White, Jr./Index Stock Imagery

93 Field Museum of Natural History

94 ©Discover Center

98 (Bkgd) Firefly Productions/Corbis, (R) ©Peter Steiner/Corbis, (T) ©John Henley/Corbis, (CR) ©Dann Tardif/Corbis, (BR) ©Ariel Skelley/Corbis

120 Creatas

121 (T) ©Ariel Skelley/Corbis, (B) ©Paul Barton/Corbis

122 ©Wayne Eastep/Getty Images

126 ©Rob Lewine/Corbis

151 ©The Ezra Jack Keats Foundation

156 ©Brooklyn Productions/Getty Images

157 (BL) Getty Images, (T) ©Patrick Molnar/Getty Images

188 (CR) ©Comstock Inc., (BL) ©Georgette Douwma/Getty Images, (Bkgd) ©Dianna Sarto/Corbis

189 (T) ©Jack Kurtz/The Image Works, Inc., (BR) ©Gary W. Carter/Corbis

192 ©LWA-JDC/Corbis

194-196 Hemera Technologies

197 (TR) ©Nik Wheeler/Corbis, (BR) ©Paul Almasy/Corbis

199 Getty Images

200 (CL, BL, TR) Hemera Technologies

201 ©Amwell/Getty Images

202 ©Rubberball Productions/Getty Images

203 ©Rob Lewine/Corbis

Glossary

The contents of this glossary have been adapted from *First Dictionary.* Copyright © 2000, Pearson Education, Inc.

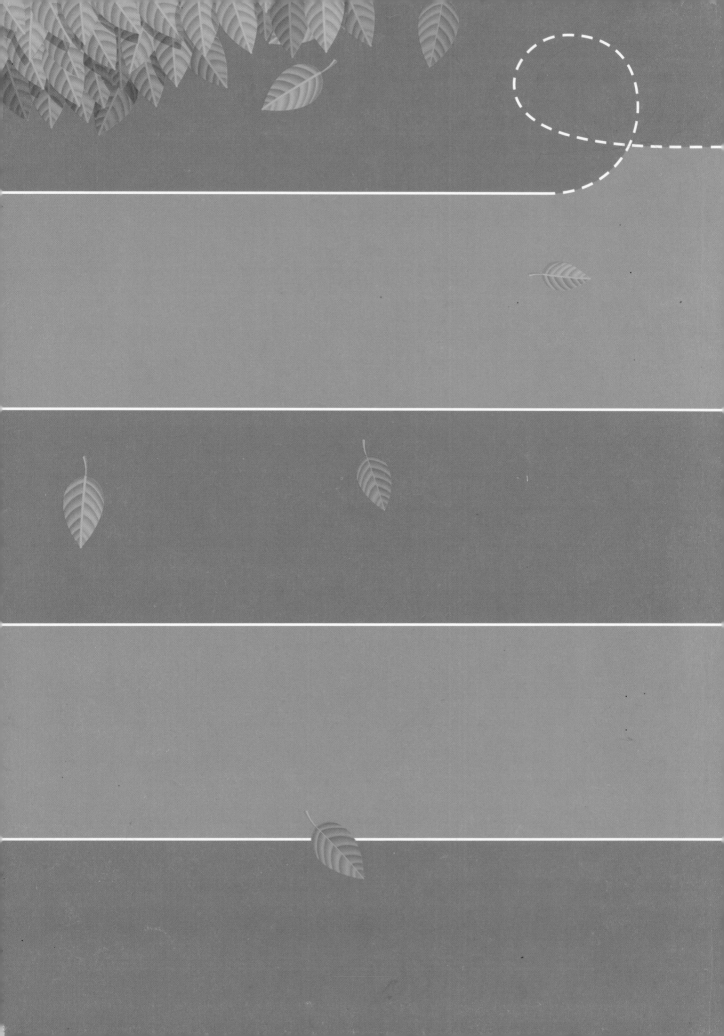